PICTURE PERFECT
POOLS

W9-AYS-930

TINA SKINNER & DINAH ROSEBERRY

Schiffer Publishing Ltd

4880 Lower Valley Road Atglen, PA 19310

Designed by John P. Cheek
Cover design by Bruce Waters

Type set in Bernard Modern BT/New Bskvll BT
ISBN: 978-0-7643-2757-5
Printed in China

Published by Schiffer Publishing Ltd.
4880 Lower Valley Road
Atglen, PA 19310
Phone: (610) 593-1777; Fax: (610) 593-2002
E-mail: Info@schifferbooks.com

For the largest selection of fine reference books on this and related subjects, please visit our web site atWe are always looking for people to write books on new and related subjects. If you have an idea for a book please contact us at the above address.

This book may be purchased from the publisher.
Include $3.95 for shipping.
Please try your bookstore first.
You may write for a free catalog.

In Europe, Schiffer books are distributed by
Bushwood Books
6 Marksbury Ave.
Kew Gardens
Surrey TW9 4JF England
Phone: 44 (0) 20 8392-8585; Fax: 44 (0) 20 8392-9876
E-mail: info@bushwoodbooks.co.uk
Website: www.bushwoodbooks.co.uk
Free postage in the U.K., Europe; air mail at cost.

Contents

Acknowledgments _____ 4

Introduction _____ 5

Spas _____ 6

Shapes and Edges _____ 17

    Rectangles _____ 17

    Contemporary _____ 24

    Free Form _____ 44

    Kidney _____ 60

    Natural Edge _____ 64

    Vanishing Edge _____ 69

Elegance _____ 87

Entertaining _____ 93

Lap Pools _____ 104

Kid Friendly _____ 109

Meandering _____ 114

Waterfalls & Water Features ___ 119

Resource List _____ 128

Acknowledgements

Many, many thanks to the wonderful designers and installation companies featured here. It's an honor to showcase your work. It is important to note that a pool environment draws on the talents of many – the engineer who makes the whole system work, the artisan who frames the pool in decorative concrete or stone, the landscaper who provides the lace of greenery, and the architect who provides a home as backdrop. Not least of all, there are the photographers who marry everyone's visions including Nature's design as the perfect cloud passes or the sun angles just so. To all, a measure of gratitude and respect.

Introduction

This book has been created to help homeowners explore a wealth of beautiful backyards from the comfort of their lounge chairs. Husbands and wives are invited on a tour that encompasses a broad variety of settings and styles, from contemporary to all-natural swimming pools, and from humble spas to expansive watering holes that thread their way throughout great backyard environments.

Though not a technical guide to terminology, this book will arm the homeowner with common language they can use with a contractor when discussing hardscaping options, pool features, and add-ons. Most importantly, though, it creates the non-verbal language needed for talking design – many images.

With this book as a tool, husbands, wives, designers, and contractors can find hundreds of examples to illustrate what they like and what is possible. Water features, edge treatments, pool shapes, and add-on spas are lavishly illustrated throughout. Grab a pad of Post-its® and set to work creating your dream backyard.

Backyard relaxation starts in the spa. These wonderful, built-in amenities heat up in minutes and you manage to wash all your stress away in even shorter order. Spas attached to pools double as water features during their down time – spilling over into pools, sending up fountains, or providing a light show. Built-in mechanisms shut-down the flow between pool and spa and speedily heat the waters when you're ready for a health-enhancing soak.

We have created sections to help you zero in on a shape or design that appeals to you. You'll find the various types of edges and shapes scattered throughout the book. These image will guide you toward the type of basic pool shape that appeals most to you and works best with your architecture and landscape setting.

Moreover, this book can act as a guide to creating a pool that will wow and impress, an attribute that can be very important for someone who does business entertaining at home. Or for someone who wants to sell a high-end home.

One section of the book explores pool settings designed with parties in mind. For those who have friends over frequently, or who have children they want to keep close at hand, this section is packed with wonderful ideas for enhancing your backyard entertaining area.

Many people add a pool for their health. A pool can be a wonderful home gym, and fitness experts wax cloquent about the health benefits of water exercise. A lap pool, or a pool designed with a lap lane, is a wonderful enhancement for someone who wants to reap the benefits of aquatic exercise.

Pools sometimes take on the role of a natural body of water in the backyard. Why should a pool be confined within the yard? Here is a selection of pools that was allowed free reign within the backyard setting, inspired by imagination.

One sure-fire way to keep the kids occupied is to provide them with water. Children love water. With proper instruction and supervision, they are the members of the family who will most utilize the pool, and it may as well be designed to channel their natural exhuberance.

For elders interested in a serene setting, a little extra thought can make the pool a meditative retreat, where the sound of water can soothe away worries and harness the attention. Fountains and jets add not only sound, but create an impressive "wow" factor. The movement of water adds a wonderful dynamic to the backyard. Water acts as a magnet, and moving water adds another dimension.

A perfect backyard escape, this stone spa has a flowing waterfall that pours into a freeform pool. When in use as a spa, the cascading water feature is switched off to allow for bubbling hot water. *Courtesy of Ocean Quest Pools by Lew Akins*

Three tiers elevate this spa above the surrounding pool creating a perfect platform from which to enjoy the natural landscape. *Courtesy of Shasta Pools & Spas*

Brick columns create a cozy setting for this contemporary octagon spa. *Courtesy of Ocean Quest Pools, Austin Texas*

Decorative tile adds visual appeal to a rounded spa with a waterspout feature. *Courtesy of Ocean Quest Pools by Lew Akins*

Situated close to the back porch, this convenient classic tile spa crowns a tile ledge that acts as a pool entrance. *Courtesy of Ocean Quest Pools, Austin Texas*

Natural stone and foliage line a pool and spa. *Courtesy of Ocean Quest Pools*

Creative features add drama to this stone spa, as water empties onto the ledge of the pool. A nearby covered waterfall directs water flow almost magically into the main body of the pool with lush landscape as backdrop. *Courtesy of Ocean Quest Pools by Lew Akins*

Sharp clean lines for this spa are enhanced by the vanishing edge of the pool and a lush forest setting beyond. *Courtesy of Ocean Quest Pools by Lew Akins*

This romantic contemporary spa and waterfall are surrounded by colorful landscaping, creating a rural retreat from the bustling city life in the distance. *Courtesy of Patio Pools and Spas*

A lavish and exciting display with water spouts doubles as a spa and serves as the perfect focal area for a patio and entertainment area. *Courtesy of Shasta Pools & Spas*

Convenient to the home, this stone spa is the ideal addition to a vanishing-edge pool. Equally convenient is the shower add-on, a great way to keep the spa clean before use. *Courtesy of Ocean Quest Pools by Lew Akins*

Fenced for privacy, this bubbling spa offers a waterfall feature that can be switched on or off, depending upon usage. An additional waterfall at the far side of the pool provides soothing water sounds, inviting the eye to move along the natural-edge of the pool, landscaped with rock and plant life. *Courtesy of Ocean Quest Pools by Lew Akins*

A nighttime view of a dreamy stone spa, the illuminating feature reflecting movement as water gently flows over the raised rock formation into the spa, and then from the spa into the pool—a visual delight. *Courtesy of Exotic Pools*

This brick spa is an inspiring addition for suburban backyard living. A facing waterfall just beyond the spa at the pool wall provides the calming background. *Courtesy of Ocean Quest Pools by Lew Akins*

Transitioning from an upper limestone deck and natural style pool, native Texas limestone boulders terrace downhill towards an expansive view of the Texas Hill Country. Native plantings including yuccas, salvias, lamb's ears, muhly grasses and sago palms lend a relaxed -- yet rugged appeal to this authentic ranch home. *Courtesy of Root Design Company*

Contemporary lines and convenient open-air style bring the surrounding landscape into the décor. Steps and ledges add to the ease of enjoying this modern pool and spa. *Courtesy of Patio Pools and Spas*

An indoor spa adds outdoor ambiance. Attractive tile, waterfall features, and green foliage complement this spa with spout, just as its location provides both convenience and privacy. *Courtesy of Ocean Quest Pools, Austin Texas*

Below:
Perfect for a smaller yard and pool, this spa with waterfall is a stylish reminder that lounging by the pool can be the ultimate relaxation. Water cascades over rocks on the opposite side of the pool. *Courtesy of Ocean Quest Pools by Lew Akins*

16

Shapes and Edges

Rectangle

An exciting family spot for relaxation and fun, this rectangular pool has a raised lounging platform doubling as a waterfall. The trellised hammock area also has a graduated entrance to the pool. Landscaping for this pool setting is very precise, mixing both stone and grass for a sculptured look. *Courtesy of Toll Brothers*

Understated elegance is the theme in this classical pool design. Simple lines and a cut-Leuders limestone terrace frame the pool while providing a generous space for comfortable entertaining and lounging. *Courtesy of Root Design Company*

A contemporary pool of rectangular shape, this classic design is the perfect addition to outdoor leisure. Flanked by a modern gazebo-like entertainment area, this pool is quietly elegant. *Courtesy of Patio Pools and Spas*

An excellent venue for entertainment, this illuminated pool and spa combine water features and a specially-designed pool entrance-way with the allure of outdoor fire to create an atmosphere of elegance and fun. *Courtesy of Exotic Pools*

The outdoor living space for this home has a brick-lined rectangular pool and covered patio as the focal point. A fire pit in the foreground invites entertaining in this backyard paradise. *Courtesy of Toll Brothers*

This stylish rectangular pool has an attached spa constructed in sculptured stone. The matching retaining wall adds both privacy and interest to the design. *Courtesy of Ocean Quest Pools by Lew Akins*

Rich, cornflower- blue reflections are an inviting feature of this edge-of-the-woodlands dark-bottomed pool. The illusion of infinite depth is achieved with a dark plaster finish. The slightest breeze intensifies the effect, adding bold ambient reflections that dance on the surface. *Courtesy of Root Design Company*

Stylish canopies create outdoor living spaces. A fire pit and several gathering areas are poolside bonuses in a backyard environment designed for entertaining. Decking and gravel surfaces combine to add visual interest and direct the flow of activities. *Courtesy of Bluegreen*

Contemporary

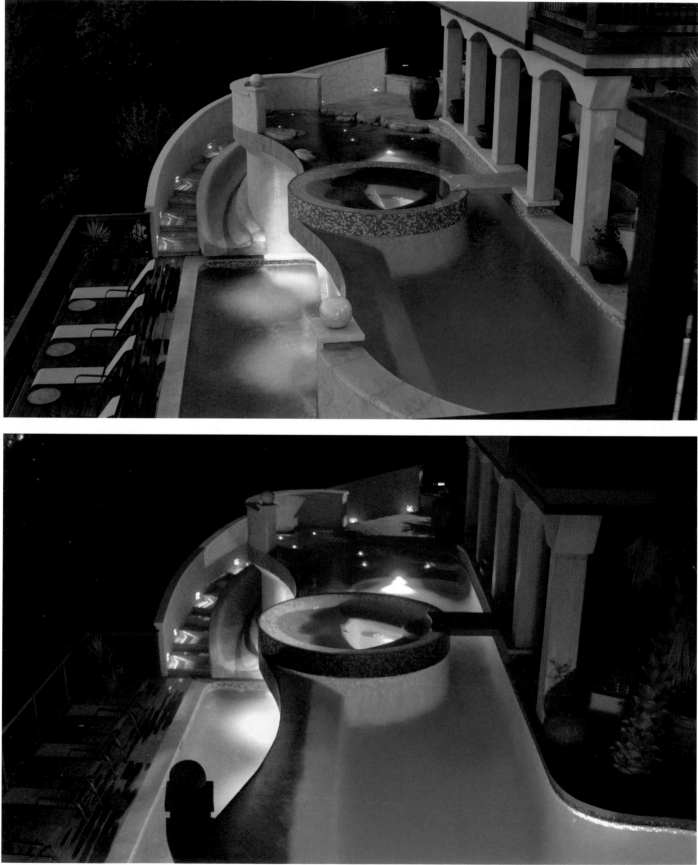

Two images illustrate two color schemes achieved with special-effects lighting. The focal point is a special walkway connecting the covered patio to the luxury spa, decorated in a varied blue tile pattern. A winding staircase, flanked by a family slide, connects the upper level to the lower level pool and lounging area. The combination of slanted, curved, and straight lines make this pool a modern family marvel. *Courtesy of Mowry Pools*

Pool and deck combine for a watery extension of the home, connecting much of the house with this outdoor play area. *Courtesy of Ocean Quest Pools, Austin Texas*

Stainless steel towers create vertical appeal, with gushing waterfalls that flow into spas at either end of the pool, which disappears into the desert with a vanishing edge. There is a spa on one corner with an underwater seating area and a table on the other corner. *Courtesy of Shasta Pools & Spas*

An elevated martini shaped spa cascades into a free-form pool with an adjacent outdoor kitchen that features custom made tile in the shape of martini glasses and olives. This family's backyard maximizes their time outside, pool-side. *Courtesy of Green Scene Landscape*

In this geometric pool with round spa, a raised decorative wall acts as an eye-catching focal point. A ledge against the wall offers cool seating area looking back at the house. *Courtesy of Ocean Quest Pools, Austin*

An angular pool is illuminated in contrast
to the darkness in the surrounding desert.
Courtesy of Patio Pools and Spas

Using the universal appeal of fire, this pool displays the warmth of flame right at pool level and behind the raised spa and cascading waterfall. The homeowners and guests can enjoy refreshments while sitting in the spa or on the other side at the counter. Whether one chooses to relax in the pool, the spa, or lounge by the fireplace at the edge of the pool, this modern venue is superbly planned. Also conveniently located right at the back door, the setting provides dramatic interest in walkway landscaping with a perfectly manicured lawn display. *Courtesy of Green Scene Landscape* *(continued on following 2 pages)*

The vanishing edge of this pool draws the eye from the pool to the lovely landscape beyond, and three flowing waterfalls provide the accompanying music. An attached spa with waterspout sits stately at the edge, inviting easy access from the nearby house. *Courtesy of Ocean Quest Pools, Austin Texas*

Falling water and jet features abound for this three-section contemporary pool, where sunbathers are afforded multi-levels for relaxation. *Courtesy of Paragon Pools*

Photography by Mary Vail, OSG

This quaint and practical contemporary pool has straight and clean lines. An attached spa with nearby lounging area acts as a magnet to lure people further into the yard. *Courtesy of Southernwind Pools, Dallas Texas*

A grand pool of geometric design, this ideal haven offers a waterfall dropping from a recycled metal mining chute and simple entrée from both the home and attached cabaña. An outdoor fireplace and kitchen with bar complete this entertainment extravaganza. *Courtesy of Patio Pools and Spas*

A simple design, this large pool has steps at the shallow end for comfortable entry and a raised decorative tile spa with waterfall for unwinding after a long day. The falls can be switched off when the spa is in use. *Courtesy of Ocean Quest Pools, Austin Texas*

Below:
The focal point of this modern pool and separate spa are the negative edges, giving the illusion of unwavering water. *Courtesy of Paragon Pools*

Photography by Mary Vail, OSG

A large rectangular spa with lots of reclining space complements this no-nonsense contemporary pool. The true spotlight is the large swimming and patio area with special brick planters and accent trims the area. *Courtesy of Ocean Quest Pools, Austin Texas*

An ideal backyard retreat, this modern pool and spa provide convenience to the nearby patio and home with easy entry to both the pool and spa. The spa offers a waterfall feature that can be controlled—off or on—for maintaining high heating temperatures.
Courtesy of Ocean Quest Pools by Lew Akins

Bold lines in pool, patio, and surrounding walls create a jet-age environment complete with water, fire, and seemingly limitless air. The two-part walkway is a wonderful statement, and adds some practicality when working with pool cleaning equipment. *Courtesy of Ibarra Rosano Design Architects, Inc.*

Freeform

This lovely free-form pool brings to mind the calming experience of lakeside views. Landscaping comes right to the edge, while various entry options are created with graduated ledges. *Courtesy of Ocean Quest Pools by Lew Akins*

The free spirit of a winding free-form pool is continued in the raised patio. *Courtesy of Toll Brothers*

Waterspouts and falls flatter this pool setting, marked by a colorful concrete skirt. *Courtesy of Ocean Quest Pools by Lew Akins*

A stonewall holds back the hill and creates a backdrop for this pool. Water trickles over rocks, into the spa, and then to the pool, bringing the freshness of the forest to the backyard. *Courtesy of Ocean Quest Pools, Austin Texas*

Decking surrounds a free-form pool and spa, and a trellis helps frame a beautiful view. A raised platform elevates the spa, which, when not in use, serves as a water feature with a spout and waterfall. *Courtesy of Ocean Quest Pools, Austin Texas*

Rocks, landscaping, and a natural shape create the sense
of a blue pond, inviting to swimmers and seemingly a part
of Nature's plan. *Courtesy of Ocean Quest Pools by Lew Akins*

In a park-like setting, this intimate freeform pool and spa is perfect for limited spaces. Trickling water over a rock wall brings the sounds of nature to this quiet, secluded backyard retreat.
Courtesy of Ocean Quest Pools by Lew Akins

A vanishing edge provides a waterfall for a lower deck, while the upper level becomes its own little world, complete with a sheltered outdoor kitchen and an incredible view. *Courtesy of Mowry Pools*

A wealth of recreation and leisure have been planned into this small backyard paradise, including a spouted spa, an outdoor kitchen, and a fire pit. *Courtesy of Patio Pools and Spas*

Simple lines define this refreshing backyard pool. The owner's love of nature is reflected in the skirt of natural rock and an ivy-covered wall. *Courtesy of Ocean Quest Pools by Lew Akins*

Enter this illuminated wonderland through a stone cave, with water trickling down from rocks overhead. Creative and inspiring, the pool lines and walkways are clean and sharp, giving full attention to the entranceway. *Courtesy of Shasta Pools & Spas*

Convenience and quiet elegance describe this free-form pool with rounded spouting spa. Inset landscaping on the patio walkway and a rock-wall soften the effect of an expansive concrete skirt. *Courtesy of Ocean Quest Pools, Austin Texas*

Below:
Wetflames™, water, and fire bowls accent an expanse of pool and spa, adding drama to a tropical backyard setting. *Courtesy of Paragon Pools*

Photography by Mary Vail, OSG

A porch spills down to an inviting pool environment, the spa rippling in invitation. *Courtesy of Ocean Quest Pools by Lew Akins*

Below:
A spectacular refuge, this pool and spa has been designed for both seclusion and entertaining. *Courtesy of Shasta Pools & Spas*

A great design for limited space, this backyard packs pool, ample patio, and a modicum of greenery into a neat retreat. *Courtesy of Ocean Quest Pools by Lew Akins*

Rock and greenery define the terminus of a yard dedicated largely to pool and patio. *Courtesy of Ocean Quest Pools by Lew Akins*

This contemporary free form pool and spa allow rock formations, segmented deck areas designed to integrate with the unstable site conditions and umbrellas to define intimate areas for sunbathing and lounging. *Courtesy of Patio Pools and Spas*

Kidney

Lighting creates drama for a pool setting in the Southwest. Accent lights illuminate selected plants, while the pool itself takes on an otherworldly glow.
Courtesy of Patio Pools and Spas

A marvelous entertainment space was created with an expansive pool deck surrounding this kidney-shaped pool and attached spa. *Courtesy of Patio Pools and Spas*

A pool exerts pull, drawing the eye, and the feet out to the far reaches of the lawn. The far side of the pool is a refreshing place from which to focus on the long view. *Courtesy of Ocean Quest Pools by Lew Akins*

A diving board is a prominent feature—but far enough away from the convenient patio to keep loungers away from the splash! *Courtesy of Ocean Quest Pools, Austin Texas*

A small pool becomes a pond-like feature within the landscaped setting of this yard. *Courtesy of Ocean Quest Pools, Austin Texas*

Natural Edge

The ideal solution for smaller outside living spaces, this pool and spa mimic Nature's design, using rock formations and landscaping to skirt a pond-like pool. Convenient to the home, yet natural enough to feel like a retreat, it fits the bill for an exciting pool design. *Courtesy of Ocean Quest Pools by Lew Akins*

This lovely pool resembles an intimate garden pond planned with rock and floral complement. The nearby patio provides the perfect lounging opportunity for this quiet and peaceful environment. *Courtesy of Ocean Quest Pools by Lew Akins*

A stonewalled wonderland, this pool displays a natural rock and foliage edge, creating a sense of oasis within the desert setting. An outdoor fireplace becomes a vertical focal point within a wall that provides privacy and a wonderful sense of security. *Courtesy of Patio Pools and Spas*

Concrete has been carefully sculpted and stained to mimic a natural rock formation, home to a bubbling hot spring, a refreshing pool, and a cascading waterfall. *Courtesy of Patio Pools and Spas*

This sparkling pool just inside a woodland area features twin waterfalls cascading off of stacked natural rock arrangements. *Courtesy of Ocean Quest Pools by Lew Akins*

Spectacular stone retaining walls make this backyard environment possible, and frame the inviting pool deck a full story below the home. The spa is nearly hidden among the realistic landscape, but looking closely, a waterfall trickles down to a basin, and then onto the main body of water. *Courtesy of Ocean Quest Pools, Austin Texas*

Vanishing Edge

Framed by the arched doorway of a covered patio, the pool seems to spill into a flowing river just beyond. *Courtesy of Ocean Quest Pools by Lew Akins*

With a modern vanishing edge design, the pool leaves the view open to the river below. A similar panorama can also be enjoyed from the wood walkway, stairs, and elevated patio. *Courtesy of Ocean Quest Pools, Austin Texas*

The all glass tile negative-edge pool seems to meld into the vast expanse of the lake beyond. The pool, with a hidden spa, appears to lunge over the edge of the shore to create a dynamic, yet extremely comfortable setting for leisurely exercise and passive relaxation. The epitome of lakeside living. *Courtesy of Root Design Company*

Two angles of vanishing edge seem to tip this pool over a cliff! It appears, too, as if the spa sits atop a peak, rather than the small elevation just above the pool. A covered lounging area and ample sunning spots compete for places from which to observe this amazing setting. *Courtesy of Patio Pools and Spas*

Photography by Lincoln Arch Photo

The glass-like sparkle of a pool reflects the home, or a contemplative visitor. The reflective effect is created using a black or dark-colored finish on the pool bottom. *Courtesy of Mowry Pools*

A well-defined slash of pool and spa seems to vanish into the sandy south-western land-scape beyond. Levels of entry into the pool or spa can be clearly seen—so lounging in the pool is as invit-ing as on the colorful patio. *Courtesy of Patio Pools and Spas*

A tongue of water projects out into the forest, three sides flowing in a smooth cascade. From below, the waterfall takes on a magical effect, the body of water suspended above its catch basin. *Courtesy of Mowry Pools*

Curves and angles outline a pool in clean clay hues, while a double-arched edge disappears against the horizon, an engineer's way of showing off. Illuminated at dusk, this pool seems to empty into the hills below. *Courtesy of Patio Pools and Spas*

A perfect example of vanishing edge and its romantic illusion. These views show a spout feature and waterfall from one angle of the pool as the eye travels over the edge into the landscape; but from another angle, that same edge seems to disappear into the body of water beyond. *Courtesy of Ocean Quest Pools by Lew Akins*

A rustic feel accompanies this lovely vanishing edge pool and spa, constructed in a location that includes nature as part of the experience. *Courtesy of Ocean Quest Pools by Lew Akins*

Still another name for the vanishing edge pool is "zero edge." A black bottom creates a reflective, glass-like surface. *Courtesy of Sundancer Creations*

An elevated negative edge helps this pool bridge the slope between home and lawn beyond. *Courtesy of Ocean Quest Pools by Lew Akins*

This pool area has the feel of a haven within a haven, as the water appears to meander over an edge and on to the beautiful view beyond. The spa with spout sits at the top of the scene with runoff from the waterfall trickling lazily through a rock passage to the pool. *Courtesy of Ocean Quest Pools by Lew Akins*

Crystal blue water pairs with the sky, forming a stunning concentration of color within the more muted tones of the desert beyond. *Courtesy of Shasta Pools & Spas*

Photography by Lincoln Arch Photo

Photography by Lincoln Arch Photo

The clean flat lines of this modern pool mimic a sheet of slate reflected in the sun. The pool has a negative edge on all sides, with suspended platforms above the water for sunning. *Courtesy of Mowry Pools*

High atop the city, this lovely vanishing edge view can be enjoyed from pool level or from the grand stone pavilion. Two waterfalls—one flanking each side of the pool—give the illusion of water being pushed along and over the edge. *Courtesy of Shasta Pools & Spas*

A pool meanders under a natural stone "bridge," offering a private soaking spot behind the elevated spa.
Courtesy of Ocean Quest Pools by Lew Akins

Three steps rise to a platform like pool, where water spills over three sides. The rock wall beyond creates a graceful terminus, at its center a waterfall spring replenishing the supply. *Courtesy of Shasta Pools & Spas*

Below:
These homeowners revel in a view of a golf course beyond the vanishing edge of their very cool pool. *Courtesy of Facings of America*

Elegance

An elegant pool with vanishing edge spa, this entertainment area combines perfectly manicured landscaping, an outdoor fireplace, and an open-air gazebo with custom ironwork.
When not in use, a spa cascades over a classically carved negative edge, the water rippling
down to the pool below. *Courtesy of Green Scene Landscape*

Classic design harkens back to the old world in a pool environment rich with ornamental fountains, a spouting spa, a columned trellis that shades lounging areas above and within the water. *Courtesy of Shasta Pools & Spas*

An arbor frames the edge of this backyard, adding style and a variety of plant materials to this pool and spa. Even the walkways around the pool were created to be permeable, allowing grass to thrive between steppingstones. A paved patio area with a custom stone fireplace and outdoor kitchen make this the perfect outdoor environment. *Courtesy of Green Scene Landscape*

Sunbathing by the side of this amazing pool will draw you into a tropical-forest haven, whether you choose to lounge at poolside, step up to the bubbling spa, relax in the outdoor gathering areas, or cook in the outdoor kitchen. *Courtesy of Green Scene Landscape*

Repeating circles and half circles stand in counterpoint to the rectangular shape of a pool. The circular tiled zero edge spa is adjacent to a warmly inviting fire pit. *Courtesy of Green Scene Landscape*

A brilliant focal point, the domed waterfall gazebo with custom ironwork creates a classic centerpiece amidst a wealth of elaboration. Further water features—a refreshing spout and striking fountain—are part of the appeal, as are the varied-level gathering areas, including a patio with an outdoor fireplace, and decorative and ornamental lighting and planters. *Courtesy of Green Scene Landscape*

Party Pools

Nothing says "party" like a Watering Hole saloon situated at the edge of a free-form, natural-setting pool!
Courtesy of Toll Brothers

A party in the suburbs is exactly what the doctor ordered with this large patio-island pool. Lamp posts ensure that the enjoyment can continue late into the evening. *Courtesy of Toll Brothers*

Below:
This lovely pool is ready to welcome sunbathers to the water-level bar with matching underwater bar stools! While guests enjoy their cocktails, they can relax to the music of a stone waterfall. *Courtesy of Toll Brothers*

What better place to host a pool party than just off the links! And this pool owner has considered the importance of varied sports by adding a basketball hoop to the pool area. *Courtesy of Ocean Quest Pools by Lew Akins*

The outdoor bar and fire pit make this pool the place to be! Water fountains and spouts add to its allure, as does the lovely mountainous backdrop. *Courtesy of Shasta Pools & Spas*

An evening gala at this pool and spa is illuminated by a romantic outdoor fire and decorative lighting. There's plenty of patio space and seating by the fire to enjoy the sparkling water. *Courtesy of Patio Pools and Spas*

No need to run inside to catch the game or a favorite show. No need to even leave the pool. If it gets chilly out, a fireplace is strategically placed to add warmth to the entertainment. *Courtesy of Toll Brothers*

An enormous outdoor recreation "room" provides homeowners with a relaxing place to lounge near the sound of falling water, or to swim in partially shaded waters. A cooking area keeps the action outside. *Courtesy of Toll Brothers*

This pool offers three-tiers of swim-able fun. The upper tier is an eighteen inch deep kids play pool that transforms itself into an adult lounge area when entertaining. Moreover, the effect is beautiful, and the cascades from one level to the next create the soothing sound of flowing water. *Courtesy of Patio Pools and Spas*

A tropical oasis, pool and spa join with nature to create a dazzling entertaining area.
Courtesy of Patio Pools and Spas

With a graduated edge for easy entry into this free-form pool, connecting to the environment is a breeze. Stone-columned pavilions also provide just the right cover for entertaining. *Courtesy of Ocean Quest Pools by Lew Akins*

Early evening by this stunning pool and spa presents the perfect outdoor ambiance. Tiled pavilions shelter an outdoor kitchen and bar and a fireside lounge area. *Courtesy of Paragon Pools*

Lap Pools

A convenient way to exercise, this lap pool is located right outside the back door, illustrating an ideal way to incorporate a pool into a small space. *Courtesy of Mowry Pools*

A beautiful outdoor environment, the pool in this scene can double as both a swimming pool and a lap pool for exercise. A large, shallow entry area is perfect for young visitors. *Courtesy of Shasta Pools & Spas*

Against a backdrop of beautiful mountains, swimming laps could not be more welcome! With a spa to help ease those tired muscles, this pool design has a real handle on managing stress! *Courtesy of Toll Brothers*

Whether lounging on the edge of the pool or swimming laps, this contemporary pool and spa provide just the right setting for combating tension. *Courtesy of Mowry Pools*

Ideal exercise havens, the lap pool and spa are wonderful remedies for a small outdoor space.
Courtesy of Bluegreen

Swimming laps and soaking in a spa are perfectly suited to the cityscape backdrop. *Courtesy of Patio Pools and Spas*

Kid Friendly

A concrete slide drops the swimmer into a beautiful vanishing edge pool. *Courtesy of Patio Pools and Spas*

Themed pool settings are very popular in family designs. Here, whales spout water in greeting. A large shallow ledge is ideal for toddlers. *Courtesy of Toll Brothers*

Photography by Mary Vail, OSG

Dolphins grace these themed pools, spreading over two levels and including a spa, too. *Courtesy of Paragon Pools*

This pool and spa are part of a backyard playground for kids of all ages! *Courtesy of Ocean Quest Pools by Lew Akins*

Take the stairs—or slide. You choose! *Courtesy of Ocean Quest Pools, Austin Texas*

110

Photography by Lincoln Arch Photo

A backyard garden provides family friendly entertainment. Lounge on the edge or step down into the pool for fun and games! *Courtesy of Ocean Quest Pools by Lew Akins*

An expansive ledge creates a wading area at the edge of a spreading pool in a park-like setting. A spa doubles as waterfall when not in use. *Courtesy of Mowry Pools*

This themed outdoor play land is complete with a rowboat-shaped spa and slide, dock patio, sandbox, and putting green, which makes this a pool party for the whole family. Kids love sneaking into the cave under the faux fort deck and water slide! *Courtesy of Green Scene Landscape*

Meandering

Passing under stone walkways, bridges, and lounging areas, this pool seems endless, its waters tantalizing as they disappear beyond the far edge. *Courtesy of Ocean Quest Pools by Lew Akins*

A pool meanders through a variety of natural landscapes, providing the illusion of a pure forest river. Combining natural and vanishing edge effects with water falls and narrow passages, anyone will feel like an explorer in the backyard haven. *Courtesy of Mowry Pools*

This pool seems to flow idly through the varied gathering areas of the property—A spa spills over, its waters flowing under a bridge before reaching the pool beyond. Poolside, a patio and bar enjoy a head-on view of a cascading waterfall. *Courtesy of Toll Brothers*

Firelight takes this vanishing edge pool panorama over the edge to the vast body of water beyond. *Courtesy of Paragon Pools*

A lovely pool with spa and fire pit fits the bill for a peaceful afternoon in a park-like setting.
Courtesy of Ocean Quest Pools, Austin Texas

Complete with a desert view, this pool boasts a water spout, natural rock dividers, and an elevated spa.
Courtesy of Shasta Pools & Spas

The evening skies reflect on the water of this tranquil and romantic scene. *Courtesy of Shasta Pools & Spas*

Waterfalls and Water Features

This stone wall doubles as a fountain. Besides acting as a visual magnet and providing the relaxing sound of falling water, the falls are part of the pool's aeration system. *Courtesy of Ocean Quest Pools by Lew Akins*

Water finds its way across rocks and into a pool that sits adjacent to a natural body of water. *Courtesy of Ocean Quest Pools, Austin Texas*

A large stone waterfall and fountain structure adorns this beautiful pool, with spillover to decorative lower levels. *Courtesy of Joyce Hoshall Interiors*

This pool enjoys a decorative wall spout and segmented waterfall fixture. *Courtesy of Shasta Pools & Spas*

Cool water flowing downhill from a stacked native Texas limestone rock formation and a separate slide cascades into the refreshing pool below. *Courtesy of Johnson Custom Pools*

Real rocks form a watery terminus for a pool in the country. *Courtesy of Ocean Quest Pools by Lew Akins*

Water cascades from a second story to the pool below. *Courtesy of Shasta Pools & Spas*

A lively fountain dances in a metal dish, elevated above the catch basin of another fountain beyond. *Courtesy of Shasta Pools & Spas*

A tranquil waterfall flows over the side of a vanishing edge pool. *Courtesy of Shasta Pools & Spas*

A decorative stone wall spills water into a natural pool. *Courtesy of Shasta Pools & Spas*

Ornamental fountains can provide restful or amusing images. *Courtesy of Shasta Pools & Spas*

Decorative tile mosaics enhance this spa and pool design. *Courtesy of Facings of America*

125

Varied rock formations and themes—both natural and decorative—channel falling water into pools. The soothing sounds of moving water and the visual calming effects are lures for most pool enthusiasts.
Courtesy of Ocean Quest Pools by Lew Akins

Resource List

Bluegreen
300 South Spring Street, Suite 202
Aspen, CO 81611
970-429-7499
www.bluegreenaspen.com

Exotic Pools
Village at Las Sendas
2941 N. Power Road, #103
Mesa, AZ 85215
480-641-2121
www.exoticpoolsaz.com

Facings of America
16421 North 90th Street
Scottsdale, AZ 85260
Main 480-222-8480
www.facingsofamerica.com

Green Scene Landscape
818-227-0740
www.greenscenelandscape.com

Ibarra Rosano Design Architects,
Inc.
2849 East Sylvia Street
Tuscon, AZ
520-795-5477
www.Ibarrarosano.com

Johnson Custom Pools
6505 Marblewood Drive
Austin, TX 78731
(512) 346-3288
www.johnsoncustompools.com

Joyce Hoshall Interiors
6608 Folsom-Auburn Road, Suite #4
Folsom, CA 95630
916-765-7538 ext. 102
www.hoshallsfolsom.com

Mowry Pools
7311 McNeil Drive
Austin, TX 78729
512-343-1066
www.mowrypools.com

Ocean Quest Pools
10208 N FM 620
Austin, TX 78726-2214
512-258-7379 ext. 117
www.OceanQuest.com

Ocean Quest Pools By Lew Akins
2606 S. I-35
Belton, TX 76513
254-933-8370
www.leakins.com

Paragon Pools
2461 Professional Court, Suite 110
Las Vegas, NV 89128

Patio Pools & Spas
7960 E. 22nd Street
Tucson, AZ 85710
1-800-my-patio
www.patiopoolsaz.com

Root DESIGN COMPANY
Landscape Architecture and Pool
Construction
1607 W. 6th Street
Austin, Texas 78703
512-459-7665
www.rootdesigncompany.com

Shasta Pools & Spas
3750 W. Indian School Road
Phoenix, AZ 3518
602-532-3788
www.shastapools.com

Southernwind Pools, Inc.
11837 Judd Ct. Ste #118
Dallas, Texas 75243
972-783-4090 ext. 1017
www.southernwindpools.com

Sundancer Creations
7 Ortiz Lane
Santa Fe, NM 87508
505-470-4365
www.sundancercreations.com

Toll Brothers
3636 North Central Avenue
Suite 1,000
Phoenix, AZ 85012
602-222-4343